Catastrophizing in Catastrophe

Catastrophizing in Catastrophe

Poems

D. E. Green

DEG

To Paul '84 and Nancy '85 (Mackey) Mueller

Here we are, nibbling
still at the yellow
tufts of nothing
before us. Making
do. Surviving. Till,
again, we thrive.

    —from "Hang Your Head"

With thanks for your ongoing advocacy of the Humanities and generous support of the Augsburg English Department.

CONTENTS

GENERAL DEDICATION   v
PREFACE   xi

POEMS 2021   1

Hang Your Head   2

Ten Haiku   3

Sonnets, Ghazals, and Pantoums   5

Sonnet: The Land of Good Intentions   6

Ghazal: Break of Day   7

Sonnet: Better Angel   8

Sonnet: First Snow   9

Pantoum: The Caregivers   10

Sonnet: Flurries   11

Sonnet: Winter World   12

Ghazal: Old Chicken   13

CONTENTS

Sonnet: Weathering Winter   14

Pantoum: Such Stuff as Dreams   15

Ghazal: Cosmic Comedy   16

Sonnet: The Cheerier Sort   17

Sonnet: Pandemic Song   18

Sonnet: The News Now   19

Sonnet: Selkies in My Bathtub   20

Ghazal: Not an Option   21

Pantoum: Joy Fills Me   22

Sonnet: On Edge   23

Villanelles   25

Villanelle 1: Winter's First Storm   26

Villanelle 2: For My Father   27

Villanelle 3: Catastrophe   28

Villanelle 4: Evening Sky in Winter   29

Villanelle 5: Dress Rehearsal   30

Sestinas   31

Sestina 1: Dangling Limb 32

Sestina 2: Draught for the Faint Heart 34

Sestina 3: Frost at Daybreak 36

Sestina 4: Viral Refrain 38

Sestina 5: Blue Notes 40

Sestina 6: In a Green Shade 42

POEMS 2017 45

Seven Haiku and a Renga 46

Two Sonnets 48

Love's Surgery 49

Raptor 50

POEMS 2018 51

On the USS Albatross 52

Paean to Compression Stockings 54

Sonnets 55

Nothingness and Being 56

Shakespeare Sonnet Pastiche: 55 + 73 57

CONTENTS

Athazagoraphobia 58

Midnight in America 59

Austerity Sonnet: Shutdown 60

Last Haiku 61

POEM 2019 63

Here at the end of the world— 64

DEDICATIONS TO SUPPORTERS OF THE AUGSBURG ENGLISH
DEPARTMENT 67
ACKNOWLEDGMENTS 69
ABOUT THE AUTHOR 70

It gives me great pleasure to offer these poems not only to general readers and lovers of poetry, but to the Augsburg community—past, present, and future—as a way to honor the donors who have so generously supported the English Department Speaker and Event Fund over the past five years. Even in the best of times, funding the humanities and arts is challenging, but Augsburg colleagues, alums, friends, and students keep stepping up to ensure that the literary arts continue to thrive and grow at the university we love.

This little collection begins with forty poems I wrote for the 2021 donors who brought us over our ten-year fund-building goal in just our fourth year. But I would be remiss if I didn't mention that we have had fantastic support from the first year of our annual fundraiser. So I have added to the current set the poems written for 2017, 2018, and 2019 donors as well. The number of poems for those earlier years is smaller simply because, before my retirement in June 2021, I had a lot less time to write as intensively as I did last fall.

You may note the absence here of any poems for 2020 donors. In Fall 2020, after several years' work with forty student editors who took Advanced Studies in Writing with me, we published a digital anthology of student writing over almost the last half century, *Murphy Square 1975-2020: A Sesquicentennial Sampler of Literature by Augsburg Students*, the link to which I sent out as a thank-you to 2020 donors. This anthology is available free to everyone through Augsburg's Lindell Library website (under University Archives).

I want to close by saying how much I have loved my thirty-three years teaching in the Augsburg English Department with so many wonderful colleagues and students. It has been a great honor.

Douglas E. Green
Professor *emeritus*
English Department
Augsburg University
Spring 2022

POEMS 2021

As I hang mine.
We are forlorn
horses in a barren
field, heads drooping
over brown stubble.

We have sad, dark
eyes. Rivers of sweat
run down our flanks,
streaking our blue-black
hides with rust-red
dampened dust.

We seem, to passing
eyes, the saddest
creatures—without
sustenance, without
purpose. And yet.

Here we are, nibbling
still at the yellow
tufts of nothing
before us. Making
do. Surviving. Till,
again, we thrive.

Ten Haiku

Haiku 1
My tires need more air.
So do I. Winter has come.
The world and I shrink.

Haiku 2
Here come the gray days:
Clouds shadow a dimmed landscape.
Then the snows arrive.

Haiku 3
I will not winter
But glide into senescence
Gracefully, greenly.

Haiku 4
Moon out at midday—
Crescent west over 4th Street—
Draws me into night.

Haiku 5
Crisp leaves brush sidewalks,
Scuttle across streets, gather
In winter's gardens.

| 4 |

Haiku 6
Hibernal sunrise
Illuminates the planet—
Iridescent love.

Haiku 7
The dark descending
A mere eight hours after dawn
Blankets sight with stars.

Haiku 8
Spring streams burble songs,
Melodies of bygone snows,
To lovers on the green.

Haiku 9
Pandemic winter
Is not unseasonable—
Streets deserted still.

Haiku 10
Summer's drought has left
The autumn evergreens gold—
Death's grove bright as joy.

Sonnets, Ghazals, and Pantoums

Sonnet: The Land of Good Intentions

In the land of good intentions nothing
much gets done. We are all old Oedipus
at Colonus, bemoaning our guilt,
our responsibility eschewing.
We didn't mean to, so we're innocent.
I prefer Lear, who shoulders the burden
of his errors: "Oh, I have ta'en / Too little
care of this! Take physic, pomp!" Lear sees what
he has done.
        The punishment may be too
severe and the motives of his raven
daughters avaricious. Nor can he now right
the many wrongs he has inflicted. At least
not on his own. We need each other kindly:
For night spreads o'er our Dover, no rescue in sight.

Ghazal: Break of Day

As I began my morning walk with the dog, the sun had not quite risen.
The night was ending. The East glowed with orange light.

But when I looked back toward downtown, the West too shone
With the soft rose of a pastel sky right after Sun has set.

We moved, the dog and I, within this doubled light—
Sunrise of this morning and premonition of sundown.

No mystery: Today Aurora had offered her rays to declining Night,
Whose departing darkness softened them to artificial dusk.

And yet. This Green world—dog and man, town and park—felt the
    universal bright,
As if in our strange time it were both break of day and fall of night.

Sonnet: Better Angel

The words echo in my head, play over
and over and over. I say them aloud,
imagine the forms gratitude and love
take: I conjure them. And revenge. I'm weak:
I can't resist taking down the enemy,
peeling back the skin of their unkindness
unkindly, rooting out the mystery
of cruelty cruelly. I could write an ode
to vengeance, a crown of sonnets to the rack,
pantoums to nail- and eye-plucking that would
shock Goneril and Regan, villanelles
to celebrate in dungeons their spilled blood:
I would sate my atavistic urges.
But I won't: I'll turn to love and gratitude.

Sonnet: First Snow

It's snowing—a crunchy white carpet,
the frigid cousin of summer's sandy beach.
This snow comes only on the coldest days.
The morning, though overcast, is lit—
even before dawn—snow refracting light
in air, and ground illuminating world.
It is so beautiful! Snow crinkles
underfoot and then across the street there
flits from bare branch to bare branch the red shock
of cardinals. The world is so lustrous!
I feel like Shelley fronting his West Wind.
Sometimes such beauty smites us, forces us
to bow before the homely deity
we've abandoned—forgotten how to love.

Pantoum: The Caregivers

We visit weekly and they're always there.
One lays out my mother-in-law's dress,
Which she selects with thought and care.
Another responds to a request for pop.

Next time we find laid out a different dress,
And Joan in the bathroom being groomed.
Then a new fellow brings in a tiny can of pop
She sips from as we sit and chat.

Today Joan has just finished being groomed.
The sun is shining through the window
As we sit. She sips her pop. We chat.
The caregivers prepare this comforting routine.

Today the sun is shining through the window
As we enter with a bag of favorite chocolates.
The caregivers move through their comforting routine.
We banter with them and admire their poise.

Again, we bring Joan her favorite chocolates.
An aide chooses a bright red scrunchy with some thought.
We banter with her as she puts up Joan's hair.
We visit weekly and marvel at such care.

Sonnet: Flurries

Here we are in winter again—flurries
embroider the edges of the sidewalks
and set off the still-green grass, tuft from tuft.
The world is enlaced, a white fog blowing
in the distance, the flakes speckling my glasses
and melting on my cheeks. Stark bare tree limbs
receive the softening down. I always forget
that winter too needs, no, demands our love.
So I will give it. I will look anew
at the world, afford it what grace I can,
seek out friends, neighbors, even strangers
to share a laugh, a stay against harsher
times—against encroaching isolation
we will seek communal consolation.

Sonnet: Winter World

The dog and I move through morning darkness,
the first dusk of day that is December.
There is snow in the air, damp and cold—wind
skinning cheeks, fingers creaking in distress.

There's nothing to be done. It's just winter.
Snow compacted into ice slips me up.
Again. I right myself and wish for spring
to lift the frigid curse we're living under.

The dark engulfs our world, far off and near,
creeps into our marrow, freezes our souls.
We cannot breathe freely, our sighs fog air
colder than the Cannon River's floes. We fear.

Hope waits on sunrise, hint of skyline bright—
a dawn I must believe rekindles light.

Ghazal: Old Chicken

Hope is perhaps the thing with feathers.* I'm not sure.
But I know it has no working wings. It pecks scraps in the yard
    and molts.

Optimism would be welcome now. A pleasant thought might cure,
If not a virus, a lot of other ills, like the spiritual mold

That mildews the soul and the eyes obscures.
No, hope no longer flies. It has no lift. It's grown quite old

And sere. It doesn't know what it's waiting for,
What arrival to expect when expectation seems far too bold.

They say hope is ever Green and will wind and rough weather endure.
But that's wishful thinking when, day after endless day, nothing new
    unfolds.

[*A play on Emily Dickinson's famous poem.]

Sonnet: Weathering Winter

Cold froze on my glove teardrops at first light,
even though I'm not one to wear emotions
on my sleeve. Frigid winter temps chilled winds
to rival my youth's worst brush-offs, their bite.

Winter tests our very mettle, seeping
through every flaw in the season's armor,
raising the hair on arms and legs in spite
of our bodies' layered wool and down swathing,

so that, even more than our minds, our flesh
yearns for spring, feels in each return to home
and hearth the warmth of the day's lengthening.
Thus we trick ourselves to begin afresh:

And thus we'll thaw, melt in each other's arms,
As if we'd ever lived so—past winter's harms.

Pantoum: Such Stuff as Dreams

Yes, *we are such stuff as dreams are made on,*
our little lives rounded with a bitter chill
that lasts months, darkens our souls slumbering
as if eternally. But sun will come,

before that bitter chill rounds out our little lives,
impending Spring draw out day's wintry hours.
We turn once more to face the glowing East—
as if eternally, Sun comes again.

Impending Spring draws out this winter day,
belated Twilight gives us leave to walk.
We turn at dusk to face the glowing West
sing hymns to morrow's possibilities.

Belated Twilight gives us leave to walk,
to while in parks our sunsets and our noons,
and sing hymns to morrow's possibilities.
We take life revived for eternity.

We while in parks our sunsets and our noons
after dark months our souls lay slumbering.
Though we take this life for eternity,
We show ourselves the very stuff of dreams.

Ghazal: Cosmic Comedy

Do not "rage, rage against the dying of the light," as the poet said.
Let your last sentence, like the one above, end on a throwaway word.

Let soup dribble down your chin onto your new holiday sweater,
just another of old age's miscalculations, betokening the end you dread.

Sip water through a straw to hydrate this shriveled body, old and
    desiccated.
Love of life is not for the fainthearted: You must anticipate the worm—

The decay of the body, of the house, of the planet. Well, not the world.
It will persist for a good long time, just not with us on it.

Some think this end a tragedy. But it's just "fire and ice," as another
    poet said.
Or something else, returning Earth to wilderness and greensward.

Sonnet: The Cheerier Sort

Would I were one of the cheerier sort,
I'd be popular, have many more friends.
A lot more folk would then with me consort,
this party or that cocktail recommend.
Were I a member of the cheerful crowd,
I wouldn't be here worrying a poem
into the world, reading each line aloud
again and yet again, till it strikes home.
But those smiling people and their laughter
simply aren't for me. I like to sit and cry
now and then, to mop my tear flow after
a melodrama, for real or on TV.
Make no mistake: I am no misanthrope.
I love this busy world—beyond all hope.

Sonnet: Pandemic Song

I'm calling it off with my friends. Again.
The risks are much too great. Covid-19
doesn't mess around. And that omicron—
it's quick. Inevitable. I don't like

this feeling that no matter my routine
or how I agonize each choice I make,
it's always wrong. A moral quandary.
I want to see my family, everyone I love.

Heck, I need them—to feel alive, to see
some purpose in my living, some intent
to act as if I knew the meaning of
love. Yet I'm calling it off with friends.

Again. The risks remain—they're still too great.
My premonition is we're just too late.

Sonnet: The News Now

Every morning I wake to the news.
It's sometimes a disaster, far or near,
the cataclysmic climatic kind—fire,
flood, tornado, hurricane. Other times

it's social—another school or police
shooting. Often now it's pandemical.
There's just no escaping catastrophe,
at least the threat of it. You live, you'll die.

Some have always lived so, have always had
to live so, for generations. You know,
driving while black in America has
never been just driving, especially

while black and male and youngish. It will maul
you—such danger. Worse than viral aerosol.

Sonnet: Selkies in My Bathtub

When I was a girl, I imagined selkies
inhabited my bathtub. I'm not sure
how they got there, but they never failed me.
I'd run the bath, get in, and there they were.
Sometimes they appeared miniature seals,
at others they seemed everyday mermaids,
and sometimes they had a dual appeal—
feral sea creature below, princess-made
above. They could be a little ominous—
at first I wasn't sure if they would bite.
They didn't, so I never had to fuss.
Skittish, they were hard to hold back from flight.
They still seem real to me, whether lies or truth.
Now they're gone—flown off, farther than my youth.

Ghazal: Not an Option

My dog barks too much—a yap so shrill it makes me doubt my selection
of this canine friend, indeed my very sanity.

But a miniature poodle—how can I blame him? I elected
him, chose him. To regret the choice now would reveal a moral laxity.

When I first encountered him, of all pups he was the model of
     precaution,
crawling on his belly to approach anything unknown like a suppliant
     devotee.

It betokened, I thought, obedience. But like our dogs we have imper-
     fections:
We are hounded by the incessant yips of our beloveds' humanity.

Regret, however, *is not an option. Because love is bigger than perfection;
it is the embracing*, ever green, *of a whole, more complicated reality.**

[*Adapted from Molly Beth Griffin's essay "The Exact
One I Wanted" in *Queer Voices* (p. 92)]

Pantoum: Joy Fills Me

At dawn peach rose-petal auras and pure
baby-blue stripes ribbon a cloudless sky.
Joy fills me—the colors, the dog's canter.
Everything betokens happiness.

Bright baby-blue pervades the noontide sky,
blinds strollers through parks, drivers on boulevards.
Joy fills me still, colors the day: I canter—
a pup, thoroughly alive, exuberant.

Blind strollers through parks, drivers on boulevards—
I feel what they feel, blood pulsing joy
like a pup, so alive, exuberant,
I want to bark and howl at brilliant moons.

What others feel, I do—blood-pulsing joy,
the wails of grieving loss, the song of Sun.
O, let us bark and howl at brilliant Moon!
Let us trill delights, sigh lamentations.

The wails of grieving loss, the songs of Sun,
at dawn raise auras, peach-petal and purple.
We have trilled delights, sighed lamentations—
Let Joy now fill, now color us—set hearts acanter.

Sonnet: On Edge

The yellow-orange glow of breaking day
traverses westward-stretching cloud-ribbons.
Light moves, it is moving, it's moving us
even at sunrise west with the declining sun,

which will go down, sink below the horizon,
to hide beyond the vast waste of ocean.
Time's order seems thus to our lying eyes,
which cannot see what intellect discerns—

how Sun rules Earth, how Sun at center flames.
Our peripheral nature makes us human,
border-dwelling, living on the margins,
rather than at the center of this system:

Such liminality spins us out far,
tangent shooting toward a distant star.

Villanelles

Villanelle 1: Winter's First Storm

The day begins with anticipation—
Snowflakes and slate skies presage its finish:
First hibernal storms foretell the season.

At the start, there's irrepressible elation:
Will this snow perfect our winter wishes?
Such days begin with anticipation.

But already we hanker for cessation,
Regret our joy, hope the flakes diminish:
First hibernal storms foretell the season.

Whirling white induces hibernation,
We nap and drowse as winds flap and whish.
Yet day began with anticipation.

The storm portends several days' stagnation,
A prospect in which we take no relish:
First hibernal storms foretell the season.

This stormy day ends in irritation
Now the dawn of our delight has vanished:
The day begun in anticipation—
This first hibernal storm—foretells the season.

Villanelle 2: For My Father

What is a father? The role keeps changing.
You cradle this stranger, squalling at you.
You're unprepared, always rearranging

Your plan. But there's no plan. You're exchanging
One task for another—painting rooms blue,
Pink, gold. What's a father? The role keeps changing.

You find emotions swing, feelings ranging
With the baby's temper and your spouse's mood—
You're unprepared, always rearranging

Your several selves. You sense them moving, ranging,
Striving to fulfill love's need, to renew
What *father* is even as it's changing.

Paternal obligations are estranging
You from whom you love and from who loves you.
You're unprepared, always rearranging

Your world, surrendering control, engaging
The strange newcomer and the one who chose you.
What's a father? The role's ever changing—
You're unprepared, always rearranging.

Villanelle 3: Catastrophe

"Don't catastrophize," my shrink counsels me.
A sigh arises from my depths: *Can you*
Catastrophize in a catastrophe?

We've been imprisoned, unable to see
Each other in the flesh. That's why we're blue.
"Don't catastrophize," my shrink counsels me.

We steel our spirits for adversity,
Force our fearful selves somehow to eschew
Catastrophizing in catastrophe.

But now we are apart, virtually
Restricted, engaging solely on Zoom.
"Don't catastrophize," my shrink counsels me.

You have sworn always to abide with me,
To keep to me, as I to you, still true.
Let's not catastrophize in catastrophe.

The pandemic rages on and on and we
Wonder daily if at long last we'll pull through.
"Don't catastrophize," my shrink counsels me
As I catastrophize in catastrophe.

Villanelle 4: Evening Sky in Winter

Winter light pastels the evening sky,
Deep orange bleeds up into pale yellow—
A palette that may soothe or terrify.

Impending dark compels we question why
Chill winds with such ferocity do blow
Though winter light pastels the evening sky.

Beauty so radiant should mollify
Our qualms and fears, the fading afterglow
A palette that should soothe, not terrify.

The luminous heavens should testify
To some Great Comfort all too seldom shown
But when winter pastels the evening sky.

Or so some do believe. Others just sigh,
Roll their eyes, think the promise hollow—
Heaven's palette neither soothes nor terrifies.

Many keep searching still for Truth on high,
Some Great Power behind the dusky glow.
When winter light pastels the evening sky,
Its palette will some soothe, some terrify.

Villanelle 5: Dress Rehearsal

Daily life is not a dress rehearsal
for living, but itself the performance.
We're onstage now, before the grand dispersal.

There's no practice run to perfect lines and all,
no backstage where we wait in dormancy.
Daily life is not a dress rehearsal.

It's our being—the here and now is all
we have. We can't appeal for clemency.
We're onstage now, before the grand dispersal.

Let's not wait, but act, not be too careful
nor stymied by striving for importance—
our daily life isn't a dress rehearsal

for something better, something magical.
Of life perfected no one can inform us—
we're onstage now but will soon disperse, all

dissolve into the ether universal,
mere elements amid a cosmic dance.
Life's simply not a dress rehearsal,
we're on the stage now, just before dispersal.

Sestinas

Sestina 1: Dangling Limb

Today I saw a broken
branch hooked overhead
on a power line
as I crossed the street.
I felt powerful and vulnerable
at the same time. It was wonderful.

It was more than elation—I felt wonderful.
They had pummeled my ego, but I hadn't broken.
I wasn't a superhero, but I wasn't vulnerable
either. I was just dangling like that branch, overhead,
just hanging high above, twisting in the wind above the street.
Nothing would cushion my fall, should I drop from the line.

It's funny: I had come from a noble line
of immigrant movie moguls, too proud but wonder-filled,
who took for granted, as if they owned it, the very streets
they walked to work and back. They couldn't imagine being
        broken—
that condition befell only those who got in over their heads.
But we wouldn't be those people. We weren't vulnerable.

No, if need be, we could dine on the vulnerable,
make them our feast if they wouldn't toe the line.
You can take a poor man and dangle possibility above his head,

make him believe in you and in himself, convince him he's wonderful.
For you he'll undertake hard labor, even murder, before he's broken,
before he lies naked, his children starving, his home a filthy street.

That's what I was thinking this morning on the street,
a delicate long branch above, so beautiful and vulnerable.
What had it been in its full glory on the tree, before the winds
      had broken
it off, before it had balanced on the line
like an acrobat on the high wire, a wonderful
sign of something grand we can't quite fathom overhead

because it's beyond us, over our head,
not just a marvel above the street,
not just a wonder full
of possibility, not just a thing in its majesty but something vulnerable,
something toward which we do not incline—
a sad thing, a thing life's broken.

We too are broken, dangling overhead
on a powerline, just above the very street
on which we think we live, so vulnerable and yet so wonderful.

Sestina 2: Draught for the Faint Heart

Like you, I live in a body,
a state not for the fainthearted.
It requires regular maintenance, like a house
or a car, so each night
it rests from the day's frenzy and rage,
when from the cup of dreams it sips

sustenance. A mere sip
suffices—gives the body
the strength it needs not to rage
like a toddler nor to turn fainthearted,
withdraw into internal night,
wander through a darkened house.

At their best our bones and flesh house
spirit, drink deeply of the world, soul-sip
the pleasures of each place, each day, each night.
Why do we not luxuriate in the body?
Why are we, in the face of such magnificence, fainthearted?
We should against the forces that constrain us rage,

should unleash our rage:
not submit meekly to house-
arrest, self-convicted, faint of heart,

afraid even to take a sip
of freedom, to unbind this body,
loose it to the liberty of night.

The nectar of sweet freedom and the night
release us from our rage
at constraints on and by the body.
We move through and beyond this human house
into the world, from which we sip
to revive our fainting hearts,

from which we faint hearts
a draught of night
can liberally sip,
can end our futile raging,
and find instead a house—
the home that we name *body*.

Though the body faints, its heart
houses the myriad powers and gifts of night:
Let it rage against constraint nor fear from the cup of liberty to sip.

Sestina 3: Frost at Daybreak

At the park it appears first to my eyes on a nearby fir,
then coats every bare branch and evergreen needle in the frost
down with which on cold days winter fog blues
the landscape. The world becomes a dream.
The soft frozen mist silvers the air,
sends down the casual stroller's spine a chill

that thrills the spirit, and not the chill
that horrifies the terrier's fur
when wind hustles the winter air.
In childhood we would with our warm breath frost
a winter pane and etch the name of one we'd dream
of, our someday love, revealed only till the wind blew

and disappeared the name. But we weren't blue,
nor daunted by the wind's deep chill.
We did not repent our dream
nor give up the hoped for
consummation. We faced the frost
of loves who saw no worth in us, who put on airs

so grandiose that they sucked the air
out of the heaven's windy blue
and covered over every thought with frost.
A haughty idol's unresponsive chill

could not undo the pleasure of the dog's soft fur
or muffle the persistence of our myriad dreams.

So we keep dreaming,
draw deep breaths of the open air
to sustain ourselves for
whatever may come out of the bright blue
winter sky, like the crystal chill
of this morning's coat of frost.

I look again at the frosted
tree limbs, silent as a winter dream,
as a stream chilled
to white ice, the air
so cold the ice looks as blue
as the spikes of a Douglas fir.

This silver world we've waited for, this frost
that doesn't blue the heart but lets it ever dream,
the still music of this winter air revive our spirit's chill.

Sestina 4: Viral Refrain

Each day I wake to the news,
always a disaster—some fire,
an obliterating flood.
Always the same sensational refrain—
one more police or school shooting,
the unstoppable coronavirus.

In my neighborhood the virus
dominates the news.
We haven't had a shooting
in some time. We're fired
up over who'll win the weekend game. We refrain
from worry over hot Decembers, odd off-season floods

in Florida. But waves of anxiety flood
through me, as noxious as this virus:
From nightmares of destruction I can't refrain.
Catastrophe has become old news,
just one more wildfire
taking down another forest, just one more shot

endangering another species—and our own. Our phones shoot
footage of another fatal traffic stop. The images flood
over us, shocking to most, flames of a daily fire
to others, a centuries-long viral

pandemic of injustice. Once novel, Covid-19's no longer new,
just one more headline, one note in a constant refrain

about disaster, illness, and death. We weary can't refrain
from soul-deep suspiration: Will green shoots,
as the seasons turn, spring forth anew?
Will April rains over parched fields flood?
Must we still despair the virus
will ever cease to burn, Pandemic's blazing fire

shrink to embers, a smoldering coal fire
we need no longer fear? How do we refrain
from paralyzing terror? Remember: pandemic viruses
do not last forever. Like shooting
stars, they may betoken disaster—this flood,
that hurricane. The sensational headlines of our diurnal news.

We cannot let such news snuff out the fire
of possibility within us or divert the flood of hope, our soul's refrain.
Let us, rather, take one more shot—and let our love alone go viral!

Sestina 5: Blue Notes

Northern winter offers another spectacular sunrise:
Creamsicle orange interwoven with baby blue
brighter than Paul Newman's eyes.
Such beauty comes unexpected, unhoped
for, like birdsong on a frosty morning, like joy
in difficult times. But there it is—stunning.

The colors saturate the sky. It stuns
us—this tie-dyed blue-orange sunrise—
right into forgotten joy.
It's impossible to feel blue,
to exile the hope
that fans out prismatic before our very eyes.

After all, love made these eyes
that witness the miracle of first light, so fleeting yet stunning.
Love always breeds hope—
even when it fails. Every sunrise
brings possibilities. Whether slate gray and overcast or clear blue,
dawn always promises a new beginning, the joy

of a fresh start, the chance to enjoy
whatever dances before our eyes:
heaven's clerestory blue,
the smile of a friend, whose face still stuns

us, a toddler son's rising
early, entering his parents' room, hoping

today to be taken in, hoping
for that tumbling or tickling joy,
that animal release, as unpredictable as the exact moment of sunrise.
We eye
the brightening horizon, stunned
by the pulse of light and the purity of blue

as perfect as Lady Day's blue
notes, the paradoxical music of hope.
It's no wonder we're stunned
by the world's joy.
even when our eyes
miss it. No, sunrise

isn't always stunning. We don't enjoy
every day the hope our eyes
seek ever—bluing sky of sunrise.

Once upon a time
is over. It's raining
again. The clouds have opened,
a downpour—the drops ping their song
above our heads, housebound
as we are, awaiting the greening

of the world. I want to transform it all *to a green
thought in a green shade.*[*] Now. To take time
by the shoulders and insist on the bond
I understood between us. I want to rein
in the present dirge and hear a happier song
wafted through the summer air across the open

fields. Right now nothing feels open—
the very possibility of fertile green
hopes seems yesterday's song.
The drops ping. I time
their plunking overhead. The rain
should feel like a gift that binds

us together. And aren't we bound
to one another? Mustn't we open
ourselves to the rain,
to the possibility of greener

worlds, more joyful times,
when the music of earthsong

will raise our spirits singing
themselves of the harmonic bond
of creature to creature from times
more distant than we can imagine. Open
your heart, love, I want to say. The green
will come again, will reign

over the fields and forests. The rain
does not signal an end—if we hear its song.
It moves the world and us into those green
thoughts that one life bind
to another, that open
our hearts to beating time.

Our pulse keeps time, like those drops of rain
we hear now. Let's open ourselves to that song,
hear in it what binds us to this life, ever green.

[*From Andrew Marvel's "The Garden"]

| 44 |

Seven Haiku and a Renga

Haiku 11
Another pewter
sky—one more day falls like lead.
In my heart, autumn.

Haiku 12
The ferns have withered—
brick-hard earth and dark and you:
leaf-dust in my hand.

Haiku 13
Medieval sky—
Blue—sunlight and atmosphere—
Autumn's sacred space

Haiku 14
Daylight diminishing—
Less light, no light—darkening—
Hunger cerulean

Haiku 15
Drizzle at sunrise—
Fallen leaves strewn across the yard—
Then—a child laughs

Haiku 16
In long-shadowed days—
Sunlight—an aperitif—
Then darkling—the night

Haiku 17
Arctic moon—clear sky—
Shadows on snow-stippled yards—
A branch cracks—echoes

Renga-style Verses

Cold—distant—like night
Your hand grazes mine—retreats—
Imagine our lips

    You flinch—in sleep—turn away—
    Could you now be—dreaming—me?

Phantom—I dream you—
Mind haunting heart's obsession—
Will you sing—with me?

    Rain troubles the lake's surface—
    Hear its song—the notes we miss

Two Sonnets

Love's Surgery

I was looking for a good person, and yet
not greatly good—anyone in a pinch
might do, who'd look at me with loving eyes
and recognize that core so clenched
the coil would not to touch untwist
but require inordinate patience,
the operation of love's exacting
surgeon, expert passionate persistence.
And there you are—scrubbed, uniformed, and masked
for the procedure: Your scalpel ready
to cut me to the very heart. No time
for anesthesia. No time for thought.
I can see only your eyes, flashing green:
You adjust the light—breathe—commence your task.

The president of fowls feathers his nest
with blood-stained quills and down of lesser birds.
He roosts under the eaves of humble homes
and caws nightlong his own magnificence.
Sparrows and wrens we harbored in the past
succumb to the predations of this jay:
His orange crest depopulates the yard.
Muted fear over bush and branch he casts.

Why don't we chase this winged rapacity
out of our gardens, bushes, eaves, and trees?
Why have we not his bloody nest ripped out
and tossed, abandoned, on the compost heap?
Do we no longer hope for the return
of birdsong and the capacity to please?

POEMS 2018

On the USS Albatross

This is our ship
        various as a city
        intimate as a village
        less like a nation
        more like a world
        with all the possibilities
        of neighbor and friend

This is our ship
        swift in the currents
        winds behind us
        but in frigid seas
        and dark wintry North
          it grinds through
          excruciating ice

This is our ship
        We will not get another

If we cannot pull together
          our lips will dry and split
          our tongues crack and swell
          our ears blister shut

We will lose our way
      our fragile home
      each other and ourselves

But this is our ship

We do not have to drown
      nor to die of thirst on these ironic waters

We can traverse these seas together
      Together we can reach our ports of call

This is our ship
      We do not need another
      We will not get another

This is our ship

Paean to Compression
Stockings

Chronic pain held you hostage
for months. Touch had fled
into exile. But after the hip
replacement, your compression
stockings brought us back
together. Those tight black
knee-highs—I had to work out
the wrinkles so that the flow
of your blood would not be
constricted. I loved kneading
your calves. I loved needing
you. I loved those socks.

Sonnets

Nothingness and Being

Does Death ever get out of the wrong side
of the bed? turn to the wall and wonder
whether it's all worthwhile? sit up and scratch
his head, lie back down—covers pulled high to hide?

Is Death like us—exhausted by routine,
day in, day out, showing up unwelcome
on your doorstep or mine or theirs, longing
for a break, a holiday? Why then so lean

and mean, slave to quota, ledger, numbers?
Consider rather what existence means,
the relevance of Descartes' *cogito*,
Berry's simple life, the taste of cucumbers.

After all, Death already knows or should:
Your stuff stays here—and only here is good.

Shakespeare Sonnet Pastiche:
55 + 73

Not marble, nor the gilded monuments
Of princes, may you *in me behold.*
No, **you shall** burn **more bright in these contents:**
My *yellow leaves, or none, or few, that cold*
Does *shake,* **shall not outlive this** paltry **rhyme.**
My *bare ruin'd choirs, where late the sweet birds sang,*
This **unswept stone besmear'd with sluttish time,**
By and by black night will *take away:* No pang
At **statues overturn**ed, **the work of masonry**
Rooted **out,** *the sunset fading in the west.*
Lost, **the living record of** my **memory.**
Then *Death* its*elf* will *seal up all in rest.*
Yet in you I see *the glowing of such fire*
That Death cannot but in its heat *expire.*

Athazagoraphobia

Most poets probably have it—the fear
of being forgotten, overlooked, ignored:
Amid red, gold, and orange, leaves brown and sere.
Against flamboyant figures, flat-fall'n word.
We want to live forever, starting now,
to seem to all around us memorable,
to unscrew inscrutable whys and hows,
and thus secure best seats at culture's table.
But such anxiety isn't ours alone:
We've siblings in our fear to go unseen,
to pace the little realms we do not own,
then disappear as if we had not been.
So poets monarchize the blank white page:
through dazzling metaphor, eternally onstage.

Midnight in America

Once there was *something better down the road—*
or so we thought. After the fallen towers,
still at war, we inched our way toward hope.
We never got there, fell to other powers.
It's dark here now. The old border between us
and them evaporates, a mere illusion—
no difference between America
and there. Day is night and all's confusion.

Once we asked, *What if the mightiest word
is love?* Not anymore. We cannot see
each other in the darkness, miss the human
touch, the neighbor's hand, the gesture—kindly,
warm—of fellow feeling. But still we yearn
for light, for life, before the silent urn.

*[The italicized phrases are from "Praise Song for the Day,"
the poem written and delivered by Elizabeth Alexander at
the 2009 Inauguration of President Obama.]*

Austerity Sonnet: Shutdown

You worked. Now you don't.
They paid you. No more.
You wonder, "Who am I?"
You're stuck at the door.

Your kids are like ours,
their needs still persist:
No home, clothing, food—
You're feeling remiss.

But you're not the problem:
You work hard every day,
tend to your duties,
and keep want at bay.

Trumped's what you've been,
And Trump's is the sin.

Last Haiku

Haiku 18
lead sky—damp umber
leaves punctuate road and walk—
dirt-black fields lament

Haiku 19
an eagle circles
plummets roadside—talons first—
scattering fat squirrels

Haiku 20
Clouded vault, endless gray—
Oh, for the light! for the blue!
A world illumined!

Haiku 21
ice-whitened branches
silvered air and crystal fog
pristine hush of Death

Haiku 22
Sun-warmed December,
Wings whoosh in arbor vitae—
Birds are still singing!

Haiku 23
Dusting of snow—light—
glows midnight—phosphorescent—
your hand—warming—mine.

Haiku 24
Wintry discontent
no inglorious summer
soothes—dark glacial night.

POEM 2019

Here at the end of the world—

announced daily by the media—
it's nice to know that we still
have each other, that we can
look across the quad and find
meaning and people we care
for. Yes, the planet is baking
and flooding, freezing and frying,
and, if we don't do the right
things in short order, so will we.

But those researchers toiling
in the labs, those writers
and readers among the library
stacks, those faces upturned
in debate, those neighborhood
meal-bearers and tutors offer
a hope, a hint, that tomorrow
is, even now, a possibility.

"Hang Your Head" (2021) *for Cheri Johnson, Lisa B. Lapka, Patricia Fox, Thomas Marshall, Laura EF Lee, Carla Steen and Jeffrey Friedl, James and Caroline Holden, Jayne Carlson*

TEN HAIKU (2021) *for Virginia McCarthy, Margo Ensz, Tracy J. Sundstrom, Scott Bibus, Matthew Green, Cass Dalglish, Rebecca Ganzel, Michael Wentzel, Cary Waterman, Mary Kay and Larry Rop*

SONNETS, GHAZALS, and PANTOUMS (2021) *for Jody Scholz, Phoebe Johnson, Eric Browning-Larsen, MLT, Mel Freitag, Charles and Nancy Maland, Madelyn Browne, Davis Jones, Catherine Nicholl, ELS, Kathryn Swanson, Pamela and Frank Sinicrope, Ronald Palosaari, Betty Christiansen, JoEllen Doebbert in honor of Belvin and Connor Doebbert, Kathleen Nybroten, Anthony Bibus III, Linda and Gerald Phillips*

VILLANELLES (2021) *for Riley Conway, Kevin Shutes, Paul Hallgren, Devoney Looser, Grace Sulerud*

SESTINAS (2021) *for Diane Palan, Peter Wodarz, Chris Scribner, Paul Kilgore, Alejandro J. Herrera and Morris Floyd, Rodney E. Hill*

SEVEN HAIKU & A RENGA (2017) *for Jessica Fanaselle, Phoebe Johnson, Matt & Allison Broughton, Devoney Looser, Catherine Nicholl, Pat Noren Enderson, Kevin Shutes, Heather Riddle, Sharon Rolenc, Margaret Erickson, Cathy & Rich Powers, JT Pinther, Jim Cihlar*

SONNETS (2017) *for Peter Wodarz, Cass Dalglish*

"On the USS Albatross" (2018) *for Devoney Looser*

"Paean to Compression Stockings" (2018) *for Kevin Shutes*

SONNETS (2018) *for Kathy Swanson, Cathie Nicholl, Phoebe Johnson, Sherri K. Larson, Garry Hesser and Nancy Homans, Tracy Sundstrom, Rebecca Ganzel, Matt Beckmann*

HAIKU (2018) *for Anonymous, Heather Riddle, Cass Dalglish, Suzanne Stenson O'Brien, Virginia M. McCarthy, the Family of Rich & Cathy Powers, Annie Lydia Dier*

"Here at the End of the World" (2019) *for all donors in 2019*

ACKNOWLEDGMENTS

"Ghazal: Old Chicken" received an *Agates* Award of Merit from the League of Minnesota Poets in Fall 2022.

"Sonnet: Better Angel" appeared in *Lost Lake Folk Opera*, Summer 2022.

"Villanelle 2: For My Father" appeared in *Third Wednesday*, Summer 2022.

"Sonnet: Winter World" and "Pantoum: Joy Fills Me" appeared in *Willows Wept Review*, Spring 2022.

"On the USS Albatross" appeared online in *Writers Night (March 2019): Resilience and Sustainability*, in the archives of the Northfield Poet Laureate's page at the Northfield Public Library website, Northfield, MN.

Several of these poems appeared in Augsburg's student-run literary magazine, then called *Murphy Square*, between 2018 and 2020.

Versions of some poems, most notably "Hang Your Head," appeared in the online monthly *Visual Verse*.

Cover Image: D. E. Green

D. E. (Doug) Green

D. E. (Doug) Green taught for 33 years in the English Department at Augsburg University. He has published articles on Shakespeare, general-interest essays, and poetry. His poem "Gratitude" won the 2018 *Martin Lake Journal* Bookend Prize; other work has recently appeared in *Bright Light: Stories in the Night*, an annual collection of poems and artwork from Southeast Minnesota (2021 and 2022); in the 2021 and 2022 *Red Wing Arts Poet Artist Collaboration*; in several issues of *Willows Wept Review*; and in *Lost Lake Folk Opera* (Summer 2022). You can also find his poems on the sidewalks of his hometown, Northfield, MN. His first collection, *Jumping the Median*, was published in October 2019 by Encircle Publications. Doug likes to say that he has been an occasional poet for 40 years.

Author Photo: Becky Boling